Spanking
Why
When
How?

D1193356

Spanking
Why
When
How?

Roy Lessin

BETHANY HOUSE PUBLISHERS
MINNEAPOLIS, MINNESOTA 55438
A Division of Bethany Fellowship, Inc.

Spanking—Why, When, How?
Copyright © 1979
Roy Lessin

Published by Bethany House Publishers
A Ministry of Bethany Fellowship, Inc.
11300 Hampshire Avenue South
Minneapolis, Minnesota 55438

Printed in the United States of America by
Bethany Press International
Minneapolis, Minnesota 55438

Library of Congress Catalog Number 79–54028

ISBN 0–87123–494–7

Foreword

Christian parents today are often perplexed concerning the place of discipline in the upbringing of their children. They can find sound and valuable answers in Roy Lessin's *SPANKING Why, When, How?* This is a remarkably well-balanced and complete approach to child training based on a consistent application of biblical principles. Parents will see from Scripture how to give their child the love, example, teaching, and discipline which God designed as the means of producing happy and obedient children. Especially helpful is the section which describes the five occasions *not* to discipline and the two specific areas that always need correction within a child. I recommend this book to all parents who want the best for their children.

Ed Wheat, M.D.
Author and Lecturer

A Word to the Reader

The subject matter of this book focuses on the biblical topic of spanking. However, it is important to remember that spanking is only one important aspect of child training.

The Bible instructs parents to "train up a child in the way he should go," and spanking needs to be seen in the proper context of that training. The correct training of children involves four vital areas: love, discipline, teaching and example. As these areas work together, the training of children comes into proper balance.

Love

Example	"Train up a child in the way he should go, and when he is old he will not depart from it." Proverbs 22:6	Discipline (spanking)

Teaching

If spanking is not seen in the context of the other three areas, it will be out of balance. Instead of bringing positive results it will then create a sense of hardness and despair in the home. Within the context of love, teaching and a proper example, however, spanking becomes an effective part of child training. The issues of love, teaching and example are not covered in any detail in this book, but are examined in my book *How to Be the Parents of Happy and Obedient Children.* *

The purpose of this book is to take a detailed and careful look at spanking from God's point of view in light of the day in which we live. Spanking is an area that is easily misunderstood and misused. It has become the object of great criticism and attack and is even declared illegal in certain parts of the world. Yet it is God himself who has placed such great importance on spanking. We're going to go over the passages in Scripture where He commands parents to make it a part of the training they give their children.

---

*Published 1978, Bible Voice, Inc., Van Nuys, CA 91409.

Most of the questions I receive from parents in my seminars on the subject of child training center around the area of spanking. I trust that as you read and study this important subject, the material will provide helpful answers to the *why*, the *when*, and the *how* of spanking, and that it will be a means of practical instruction and encouragement to you.

Roy Lessin
Spring, 1979

"The greatest gift a child can give a parent is cheerful obedience."
T. A. Hegre

Contents

Part One

Why Is Spanking Necessary?

A mother with a full cart of groceries struggled with her four-year-old son as they stood in the checkout line.

"Billy, I told you to stay here. You may not go over to the magazines."

"I want to." Billy jerked free of his mother's arm and ran toward the magazines again.

"Get back here right now or you're going to get it!"

"No!" Billy yelled.

Billy's mom quickly stepped out of line, jerked him by the arm and pulled him back. Billy began to holler, twisting and pulling away from her.

"Let go!"

"Shut up and stand still!" his mother hissed angrily.

Billy's behavior remained adamant.

The struggle continued until the clerk finally rang up the groceries, bagged and then stacked them in a cart ready to push out to the car. Homeward went a frustrated and angered mother and son.

A father returns home from a tension-filled day at the office only to discover his ten-year-old son has disobeyed his instructions and is playing with his new set of golf clubs.

"You good-for-nothing kid! I told you not to touch my golf clubs! Why can't you learn to listen to me?" shouted the father, cruelly hitting his son across the face.

At the main counter of the public library a woman stood in line waiting for the librarian to stamp the cards on the small stack of books she had selected. Next to her stood her two preschool children. The two children began arguing with each other. Pushing and hitting quickly followed.

"Children, stop at once! Don't you know that is no way to act?" said the mother feebly.

By this time the librarian was beginning her checkout procedure with the mother's stack of books. The children's rowdy activity caught her attention. As she gazed over the counter to get a closer look at the argument, the mother spoke up and said, "Oh, I'm sorry for the disturbance. They haven't had their nap yet today, and when they don't get their nap they are impossible." The librarian went back to her work and the mother made several more futile attempts to quiet them. When the librarian finished her job the mother gathered her books and started for the door. Shaking her head, she made one final statement to her children about their behavior. "O children, Mommy is so disappointed—*so* disappointed in you."

Parents want their children to obey them when they ask them to do something, yet many parents fail to get obedience. Some are so discouraged and frustrated they don't believe obedience from their children is even possible. After she was asked if she knew how to get children to obey, one mother responded, "The only way I know how to get children to obey is just not have any children."

What is wrong? Why don't many parents

get the results they so desire to see? Why do many parents often succumb to anger, frustration, despair or cruelty in their attempts to train their children?

When someone buys a new appliance he is provided with an instruction manual by the manufacturer. It tells one how to use the appliance and how to keep it in the best working order. If something goes wrong the customer is encouraged to contact the manufacturer for repairs. So it is with the family. The family is God's idea. He brought it into being. In His Word He has given clear instructions as to how He intends it to function. When parents experience problems in training their children, He is the one to be consulted. He has given parents the rich counsel of His wisdom to guide them in the important matter of training their children.

HINDRANCES TO DISCIPLINE

Many of the problems and failures parents experience in training their children are a result of not seeking God's wisdom and instruction and applying it to their lives. There are several hindrances which keep parents from receiving God's wisdom and instruction in the area of discipline.

Humanistic Thinking

One of the hindrances to discipline is humanistic thinking. Often this philosophy carries the idea that parental authority and discipline are wrong, that they hinder true freedom. The concept that children are basically good and if left to themselves will grow up to be happy, fulfilled people is another plank in the philosophy of humanism. Because this world's way of thinking has such a strong influence, even among Christians, many parents become skeptical of discipline and feel they will hinder their children's development and future happiness if they spank them.

The Bible tells us, however, that "folly [foolishness] is bound up in the heart of a child, but the rod of discipline drives it far from him" (Prov. 22:15). "Foolish" does not here describe someone who is playful, has a good sense of humor, or is immature. Rather, this word refers to a selfish disposition of the heart that disregards God's wisdom and will, choosing to live independently of Him. "A child left to himself [left to have his own way]," the Bible tells us, "brings shame to his mother" (Prov. 29:15). It is the liberation from this selfish and independent attitude within the heart, not the liberation from parents and their authority, that brings true freedom. This freedom brings real and lasting happiness because it frees children from the guilt and bondage which selfishness causes.

It is also important to understand God's purpose in establishing parental authority and discipline in the home. He has meant them both for good. They are to be a positive and redemptive influence on children. God wants parents to give children the kind of leadership they *need*, not the kind they want. Children, with their limited knowledge and experience, are not able to discern what is good or best for them. They need to have guidelines and these come through parental authority. A two-year-old may want ice cream for breakfast, but he does not have the understanding of nutrition to know it's not good for him to have ice cream as a meal.

God's kingdom is a kingdom of love and order. It is a kingdom of right relationships. God's desire is that a family experience and express His kingdom within the home. His purpose in giving parents the place of authority in the home is not that they may then provide cruel, hard or unjust leadership. Neither is their leadership to be indifferent, careless or permissive. Rather, they are to supply the same loving, caring leadership that God gives to His spiritual children. The heavenly Father is the proper example of parental authority.

False Love

Another hindrance to discipline comes from a misunderstanding of the meaning of love. Some parents will say, "I love my children too much to spank them." On the surface this may sound good, but it falls far short of the kind of love God wants parents to show to their children.

God is love; His love desires the best and highest for every individual. Since real love chooses the best, it must bring correction to anything within an individual's life that will keep that one from the best. Without true discipline there is not true love, and without true love there is not true discipline. "He who spares the rod hates his son, but he who loves him is diligent to discipline him" (Prov. 13:24).

For example, love knows that such areas as disobedience, selfishness, anger, or resentment will cause children to fall short of God's best for their lives. Love says, "I care too much to allow that to go uncorrected."

As parents look to God as their example they will be faithful to discipline their children when they need it. As they discipline, they will be expressing the kind of love children really need. "My son, do not regard lightly the discipline of the Lord, nor lose courage when you are punished by him. For the Lord disciplines him *whom he loves*, and chastises every son whom he receives" (Heb. 12:5, 6).

It is important to remember that the highest desire any parent can have for their children is to see them come to love and serve God with all their hearts. Through proper discipline a parent is helping to prepare children's hearts to love and follow

God's will for them, and to know the joy and peace He desires to give them through His Son Jesus Christ.

Child Abuse

Another hindrance that keeps some parents from spanking their children is the issue of child abuse. This is an area that has rightly been a source of grief for concerned people everywhere. Child abuse can surface in various ways—sexual, verbal, physical and even emotional abuse. I'm sure we've all been shocked and repulsed to hear of parents who, in the name of discipline, uncontrollably strike out at their children, inflicting bodily injury even to the point of breaking bones and dislocating limbs. Occasionally extreme cases of child abuse are discovered; one report recently told of a child who had been locked in a closet for weeks, not being allowed to speak or see anyone.

Many teenage runaways are trying to escape the emotional abuse in their middle-class, materialistic homes. "But we gave her everything she wanted" is the bitter parental cry, with no conception of the caring, sharing, loving discipline that was missing.

What a tragedy when children do not have parents who look to God to provide the instruction and example they need for loving leadership. No matter what form it takes—whether it be neglect and rejection, or assault and brutality—child abuse should be despised by every parent.

However, in rejecting even the thought of child abuse, parents must be careful not to reject God's way of providing loving correction through spanking. This is not to be confused with child abuse. Parents must guard against the fear that loving discipline is a form of child abuse. And they also must be careful not to become critical and wrongly judge parents who do provide this discipline.

The *failure* to provide loving discipline through spanking is also a form of child abuse. Children need the loving correction of a spanking because it affects eternal issues as well as temporal issues. "Do not withhold discipline from a child; if you beat [spank] him with a rod, he will not die. If you beat [spank] him with the rod you will save his life from Sheol [hell]" (Prov. 23:13, 14).

The word "beat" as used in the above scripture has a different connotation in modern usage than it does in the original translation; it does not mean punching children or throwing objects at them. "Beat" means to strike, to hit with a rod, to give a spanking. It means to spank in the correct manner, not with the purpose of bringing physical damage but of bringing loving correction to a child's heart. A spanking is not a time for parents to release personal frustration, tension or wrath. "For the anger of man does not work the righteousness of God" (James 1:20). Whereas physical child abuse can result from anger, selfishness, frustration or anxiety, the proper discipline provided through spanking is motivated by love.

Though a spanking is not intended to be an enjoyable experience to a child or to the parent, if properly given it reaps positive and long-lasting benefits. "For the moment all discipline seems painful rather than pleasant; later it yields the peaceful fruit of righteousness to those who have been trained by it" (Heb. 12:11).

We were blessed with a healthy, content baby daughter. She slept, ate and cooed like she was supposed to. One day, when she was a little older, my wife went to put our daughter down for her usual afternoon nap. Suddenly, she let out the most obvious protesting cry which said "I don't want to go to bed." For several days this fuss would be made whenever it was nap time. My wife and I decided we should discipline her with a spanking whenever this occurred. In less than a week her attitude changed, the protest ended, and she went to bed with an agreeable disposition. Because this issue was corrected, bedtime became a pleasant, peaceful time for all of us instead of a time of conflict and tension.

Applying the same principle of loving discipline to other areas of our children's lives that needed correction, we experienced the same positive results. We found that obedience became a normal, expected part of their behavior. Cranky, fussy attitudes changed to attitudes of pleasantness and happiness. We found we could really enjoy our children through every phase of their growth. We didn't dread taking them places or fear their reactions to us when we asked them to do something. They became a continual reminder to us of God's faithfulness to His Word: we saw the peaceable fruits of righteousness He had promised to develop in them. This does not mean that they were perfect or that we never made mistakes. Their training required a lot of time and a lot of work, especially the first six years. But the fruit came; happiness and obedience were the result.

While discussing the difference between correct discipline and child abuse recently with a group of parents, I heard the following story. "When I was a small boy," a man said, "my father would go through periods of great anger and frustration. He'd lash out at everything around him. During some of these outbursts, I fell victim to his wrath. Often he would punch me and cause me physical injury." He went on to say, "Now that I'm a parent I find it difficult to bring myself to spank my son when I know he needs it. Whenever I've come close to the point of giving my son a spanking, I remember what my father did to me and I change my mind." This man's reaction to his father's behavior is understandable, yet he allowed this experience to push him to the opposite extreme with his own child. Neither physical abuse nor neglect of correction is what God desires for parents in the training of their children. The following illustration helped this man to clarify the balancing point in his life. Let's imagine a pendulum:

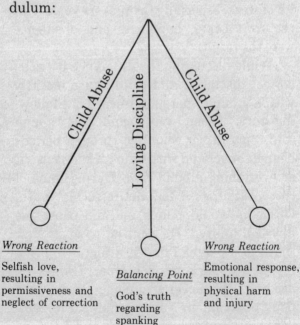

Child Abuse *Loving Discipline* *Child Abuse*

Wrong Reaction

Selfish love, resulting in permissiveness and neglect of correction

Balancing Point

God's truth regarding spanking

Wrong Reaction

Emotional response, resulting in physical harm and injury

Experiencing the error of either extreme position, one might counterreact with the opposite wrong reaction instead of moving to the balancing point of God's truth.

Laziness

Another hindrance to parents spanking their children is personal laziness. Spanking takes a full commitment of the will of both parents to make it an effective part of the training of children. Some parents have said, "I don't like having to spank my children to correct them because it's too much work." It is true that providing the loving discipline of spanking is hard work, but it must be done in obedience to God's Word. And it's worth it if the parents' goal is to see the fruits of happiness and obedience in their children's lives. Keeping a garden is hard work. It takes time to prepare the soil, plant, fertilize, water and pull weeds. But the results—a basket of fresh vegetables on the kitchen table—make the memory of the hard work fade. Spanking, too, is a necessary part of the work that's needed to see positive fruit coming from children's lives.

I will say it again: spanking is not some idea man has come up with for training and disciplining children. Neither is spanking an old-fashioned idea. Spanking is God's idea. He is the one who has commanded parents to spank their children as an expression of love. Spanking is not optional. It is an issue love cannot compromise. The question we face as parents is this: do we love God enough to obey Him, and do we love our children enough to bring into their lives the correction of spanking when it is needed? As we are faithful to obey Him in love and are careful to spank our children in a *correct way* and for the *right reasons*, we will begin to see the positive fruits that God has promised produced in our children.

Key Thought

God is the one who has instructed parents to spank their children as an expression of love.

Key Verse

"He who spares the rod hates his son, but he who loves him is diligent to discipline him."—Prov. 13:24

Part Two

When to Give a Spanking

It is not uncommon for parents who understand the necessity God places on spanking to lack understanding about *when* a spanking should be given. God has never intended a spanking to be given in a haphazard manner. It has a direct purpose and is to be given for specific reasons.

FIVE OCCASIONS *NOT* TO DISCIPLINE

Childishness

A spanking should never be used to force something upon children they are not prepared to handle because of age. Children should not be disciplined for being themselves, for acting their age. There is nothing wrong with the limitations found at age two or six or any other age. God wants parents to enjoy their children at every stage of growth. Children, refreshing and spontaneous, can be innocent and naive in their thinking, and direct and honest in their speech. They are not meant to carry the responsibilities or make the decisions of an adult. Normal immaturity is not an issue for discipline.

Lack of Ability

Parents must also guard against using a spanking to try to make their children duplicate someone else's abilities. For example, to force a child through discipline to perform equally with the athletic or intellectual abilities of a neighbor's child would be cruel and unfair. Within a family there may be one child who loves to read in his spare time. Another child may enjoy creating things with his hands. Still another skillfully plays a musical instrument. Parents should not wrongly compare their children with each other or try to force one child's interests on another child. This can create frustration and pressure on both the parents and the children. A parent needs to nurture and allow to blossom the special gifts God has given each child. Every child is unique in his or her ability, aptitude and personality.

Accidents

Legitimate forgetfulness and unintentional accidents are also not reasons for giving a spanking. Parents need to be careful to differentiate between *faultless* and *blameless* behavior in their children. Many times children may spontaneously attempt to help their parents and the motive does not match the results. One night, after the evening meal, a tired mother went out for an hour to do some needed shopping. Her two children decided they would like to surprise her by doing the dishes before she returned. After checking with their father, they set out on their task. When mother came home she was delighted to discover a clean kitchen— all the dishes washed and put away. Later that evening when she went to throw away some paper, she discovered one of her favorite glasses lying broken in the trash basket. But she knew this was not an issue for discipline. She knew that although her children

were not *faultless* in their attempt at doing
the dishes, they were *blameless* in their in-
tention.

Incomplete Information

Another time when a spanking should
not be given is when parents are not sure of
all the facts surrounding a particular incident. Do not "rush to judgment" if all the
issues are not clear. A parent should not rely
only on "hear-say" information, but should
be certain of what really took place.

One day my daughter came into the
house crying in pain, her hand over her eye.
When I asked her what had happened, she
said her brother hit her. Imagining the
worst, I called him in and began to repri-
mand him, certain that a spanking was in
order for his action. Fortunately, before I
came to the final correction I found out what
had actually happened: instead of deliber-
ately hitting her in the eye, he had been
simply bouncing a ball on the patio; it had
glanced off a rock and hit his sister in the
eye. I quickly apologized to my son for my
hasty conclusion and he apologized to his

sister for unintentionally hurting her.

Out of Anger

A spanking should not be given when a parent is responding to his child in anger. It is not for the purpose of releasing parental frustration, and should not be based on a parent's emotions. Child abuse is the result of this kind of discipline. Rather, spanking is providing loving correction on the basis of obedience to God's Word.

In order to understand when a spanking should be given, it is important to remember the ultimate purpose or goal parents should have for their children. The highest goal love can have for children is to see them come to believe on the Lord Jesus Christ as their personal Lord and Savior, and from a heart of love joyfully serve and obey Him. The secondary goal of parents, then, is to see formed within their children the positive qualities of Christlike character. A spanking is given for the purpose of helping to correct those areas within a child's life that would hinder him or her from joyfully obeying the Lord. A spanking ultimately helps prepare children's hearts to seek the highest and best God has for them.

TWO AREAS FOR DISCIPLINE

The specific areas that need correction within a child are the areas of *willful disobedience* and *wrong attitudes*. As parents train their children to obey them with a right (cooperative) attitude, they will be preparing them to obey God with a right attitude. "Children, obey your parents in the Lord, for this is right" (Eph. 6:1). The importance God places on these areas in a person's life can be seen in the following scriptures: "He has showed you, O man, what is good; and what does the Lord require of you but to *do justice*, and to *love kindness*, and to *walk humbly* with your God?" (Micah 6:8). "The end of the matter; all has been heard. *Fear God*, and *keep his commandments*; for this is the whole duty of man" (Eccles. 12:13).

The areas of obedience and right attitudes that are brought out in these verses can be seen as follows:

Obedience	*Right Attitudes*
Do justice	Love kindness
Walk	Humbly
Keep His commandments	Fear God

God expects obedience and right attitudes from everyone. Parents also should expect obedience and right attitudes from their children. These issues should be a major part of a child's training. Willing obedience from children should be expected by parents because God has instructed so. This is part of children's responsibility to God and to their parents. Cheerful obedience to parents is how a child pleases God. Willful disobedience and wrong attitudes are never acceptable and need to be corrected with a spanking.

Parents who use rewards such as money or candy to get obedience from their children are not helping to develop their children's character in a proper way. Instead of training them to obey because obedience is right and expected by God, they are being trained with the selfish concept of "I'll obey for what I can get out of it."

One day while my wife was waiting in line at a bank, she observed a mother trying to get her two-year-old son to come to her. She called out several times "Come here." Instead of obeying, the child ran off in the opposite direction. In desperation the mother said, "Come here and I'll give you a sucker." The child came to her immediately. This is not training for obedience; rather, it is rewarding the child for stubbornness.

To understand how important the areas of obedience and right attitudes are to a child's relationship to God, to parents, and to all of life, we need to look at each area more closely.

Obedience

"Children, obey your parents in everything, for this pleases the Lord" (Col. 3:20). In discussing the issue of children obeying their parents, a father once questioned its possibility with the statement, "You may have been able to get your children to obey you, but it won't work with *my* kids. They have different personalities than yours do, and obeying doesn't come naturally to them." No place does the Bible teach that obedience or right attitudes are natural responses for any child. It is disobedience that is natural. Parents don't have to train their children to lie, to rebel or get angry; but they do need to train them to obey, no matter what their personality may be.

Each child is a unique creation of God. Each child has distinctive physical features, personalities, aptitudes and abilities. Yet no matter how much these areas may differ from child to child, each one can still learn to obey.

Our son was a very active child, on the go constantly. He had to *learn* to sit still at times and be quiet. Training him to obey helped him to develop self-control. Our daughter was much more quiet and reserved, but she had a very strong will. When we asked her to come to us or told her not to touch something, she would often just stand and look at us, refusing to obey. Training her to obey helped her to overcome stubbornness. Each child required more training in certain areas, yet the issue of obedience remained the same for both of them. God has not excused any temperament or personality from His command of children's obedience. Because God places such importance on this area, willful disobedience from children becomes one of the major areas that needs loving correction by spanking.

In recognizing willful disobedience, a parent needs to understand the difference between what a child is *able* to do and what a child *will not do*. If a two-year-old is asked to vacuum but does not, this is not willful disobedience because the age limits that physical ability or comprehension to obey. However, if a two-year-old is told to "come here" but refuses and goes in an opposite direction, ignoring the parent, that is willful disobedience. It is clear to the parent that the child is able to "come here," but will not.

The Bible states that obedience must be complete. (This directive, of course, takes into account that parents will not be leading their children into areas of evil.) Children are not to obey their parents only when and if they feel like it. God wants them to respond to their parents' authority and to learn to obey them in every area. Partial obedience by a child is not acceptable and needs to be disciplined. Very small children should be given only one or two simple instructions at once. Instead of saying, "Clean up your room," one mother tells her toddler, "Put five toys in the toy box." When that is finished she says, "Now put five more in." (The youngster gets some counting experience also!)

If an older child is asked to throw out the trash and sweep the sidewalk but does only the first chore, this is not complete obedience. If children are given jobs around the house, these responsibilities should be completed (including putting away the tools for that job) before they go off to do other things.

The importance of complete obedience is seen in the story of the partial obedience of King Saul. God had instructed him to utterly destroy the Amalekites, including their livestock. When Saul was confronted by Samuel after the battle, he was asked if he fully obeyed God. As Saul uttered an affirmative reply, Samuel heard the bleating of sheep in the background. When asked about this, Saul justified his disobedience by saying he had kept them back to offer in sacrifice to God. Samuel's answer: "Behold, to obey is better than sacrifice, and to hearken than the fat of rams." The consequence of this partial obedience resulted in the kingdom being taken from him. (See 1 Samuel 15.)

Another important aspect of obedience is that of promptness. The classic injunction "Delayed obedience is disobedience" still holds true. When a parent asks a child to do something once, in a normal tone of voice, a child should be trained to obey the first time he or she is asked. Some parents may question the importance of training children to obey promptly. The main principle in prompt obedience is for a child to learn to respond to a parent's word, whether that word be "no" or a specific directive such as "Pick up your toys." As children learn to respond to simple directives when they are young, their hearts will be prepared to obey the Lord in more important areas when they are older. If a parent says to the child, "Don't take any more potato chips now; you've had enough," but three minutes later the child goes and takes a handful of chips, that is disobedience.

Parents can also fall into the trap of taking action only after continual warnings, or after reaching the point of personal anger or frustration. Children should learn that their parents mean what they say and that *they expect obedience the first time they speak*. The reason so many children don't obey until their parents have asked them four or five times or until their parents become angry and threaten them is that they have been *trained* to wait until then. The children quickly learn to know at what point their parents really mean what they say.

One mother told about how frustrated she was in getting her daughter to obey. She said she would ask and ask and ask, but get no response. Finally, in hopeless anger, she would say, "You better obey me now or you're in for big trouble." Discussing this further with us, the mother realized why she was getting a positive response from her daughter only at that point: she had trained her daughter to obey when she heard the phrase, "or you're in for big trouble." The girl knew that was the signal, the phrase which indicated her mother really meant what she said. The right way and easiest

48

way for both child and parent is training to obey at the first word. The results are a calm and peaceful home for both parents and children.

The consequences of delayed obedience are seen in the life of Jonah. He eventually did go to the place God had told him to go, Nineveh; but the price of his delay brought his life and the lives of others into great danger. (See Jonah 1 and 2.) Prompt, thorough obedience is an important characteristic of a life that pleases God. It is also vital for a child's total well-being. A parent who calls to a child about to run into a busy street expects total and prompt obedience to protect that child's life.

Children need to learn to obey their parents' word, even if another adult tells them something different. One day my wife and two-year-old daughter were visiting a friend's home. During the visit our daughter went to the coffee table and was about to pull off the magazines neatly stacked there. My wife said to her, "No, don't touch the magazines."

While our daughter was deciding whether or not to obey, our friend said, "It's okay, let her play with them."

My wife replied to our friend, "Thank you, but I've already told her no, and I want her to obey my word." When children are very young it is important to stick to what you have said so they don't become confused about what your word means. Meaning what you say is a way to establish your authority before your children.

Also, *obedience from children should be unquestioned*; it should not be based upon how reasonable a command sounds to the child. A parent's directive does not have to be reasonable to the child in order to be obeyed. Parents who try to reason with their children in order to get obedience usually wind up frustrated and outwitted; and usually they come to the place of using a bribe to get the response they're after.

A mother who wanted her six-year-old daughter to come to the kitchen for lunch called out the window, "Honey, wouldn't you like to come in and eat now?"

"No, Mom," came the reply, "I'm having too much fun."

"But, honey, think how good the food will taste."

"Later, Mom."

"Don't you think it's best to eat now?"

"No."

"Mommy has lunch all ready for you. Why don't you come in for lunch now? If you do I'll take you to the park for an hour so you can play on the swings."

"Okay, Mom, I'll be right in."

Instead of simply telling her daughter what she wanted and expecting prompt obedience, the mother tried to talk her daughter into obedience. This type of an approach, which needed a bribe in order to work, may get a response in the end, but that response cannot be called obedience; it does not train a child to obey.

Obedience means a right response not only to a parent's word but to God's Word as well. Issues such as lying and stealing also need to be corrected with a spanking. In this way parents are reinforcing the authority of God's Word in their children's lives.

Attitudes

The other major area for discipline in children is the area of right attitudes. God desires not only prompt and complete obedience but *joyful* obedience that comes from the heart. "Serve the Lord with gladness" (Ps. 100:2). This is not a fake or "put-on" outward appearance that a child assumes. Neither is it a happiness based on favorable circumstances, good feelings or getting one's own way. If children are happy only when they can have their own way, they are not truly happy. True happiness is the result of a heart choice that delights to obey. Real joy comes to children who know their obedience pleases both God and their parents.

If a parent asks a child to clean his room and the child goes about his task with a long face and a complaint on his lips, this is not joyful obedience. If a child is told that it's time for bed and the child goes to his room pouting, this is not joyful obedience. These wrong attitudes need the loving correction of a spanking. A child who fusses or whines is manifesting an attitude of ungratefulness or complaint, and this needs correction.

Children should be encouraged to come to their parents at any time and freely express themselves and ask questions, but they need to be trained to speak in a pleasant tone of voice, showing the respect and contentment that comes from a right attitude. Because right attitudes are issues of the will and not the emotions, a child can choose to be happy and content. The feelings, the emotions, are a barometer of the will. When a child chooses the proper attitude, the appropriate emotional response will follow. At mealtime, for example, a child may not like a particular food that's being served, but the child can be trained to eat it with a thankful heart. Even a small child can be told, "Please change your attitude. Be happy," and be trained to do so.

An experience I had with my son helped me to see how a parent can help a child choose to overcome wrong attitudes. When he was younger he would, on occasion, wake up from nap times with a cranky, fussy disposition. Instead of correcting his attitude, I accepted it. I reasoned it was only normal for a child to feel bad and act cranky after a nap! One day I was challenged by the comment of a visitor who happened to observe this attitude. "You know, Roy," the visitor said, "that cranky attitude doesn't have to be." As I thought about that statement, the truth of it began to register. I realized my son was acting this way because I was allowing it. By doing this I was not loving him as I should. I was allowing him to be ruled by his emotions, which were causing him to be an unhappy person after naps. I saw the need and importance for correction in this area. The next time he woke up from a nap with a cranky disposition, I said, "I know you just got up from a nap and you are still a little sleepy, but I don't want you to be fussy or cranky during this wake-up time." I found it took only a few spankings to see his entire disposition change. It still took him time to fully wake up from a nap, but his attitude was pleasant and agreeable. He actually learned to choose to be happy, and as a result of that choice he formed a new and much better habit.

Wrong attitudes in children often come to light during playtime with friends or siblings. Often these selfish attitudes will be expressed in arguing, grabbing, pinching or fighting. Children can learn to be kind to one another. When children protest or throw temper tantrums, this too is a manifestation of a wrong attitude. The loving correction of a spanking is needed in order to correct these attitudes.

A temper tantrum is not something a parent should ignore, or laugh at, or play along with in order to show the child how silly he looks. Children discover different methods for getting their own way. Some children will act cute, some will beg, others will throw temper tantrums. Some children will pretend they don't hear, others will pretend they don't understand, while others will come up with the "I-forgot-to" tactic. Children need to know that wrong attitudes are never acceptable. If these attitudes are not dealt with quickly and firmly, not only will the child become unhappy but the well-being of the whole family is affected as well.

Dad and Mom are going to take the family for an outing to Uncle Joe's farm, but six-year-old Bobby decides he'd rather stay home and go swimming. In protest he pouts and complains, "I don't want to go." While the family begins to pack up the car for their drive, Bobby continues to mope and fuss and protest. The whole drive to the farm is a tension-filled trip because Bobby didn't get his own way. Before the family arrives at the farm Bobby makes one last effort to get his own way; he throws a temper tantrum. Once at the farm, realizing his final effort has failed, he decides he will make the day as miserable as he can for everyone. Sulking and uncooperative, he manages to accomplish his goal. Everyone is relieved when it's time to go home because Bobby's attitude has ruined the fun for everyone in the family. Sad to say, this type of story repeats itself over and over in many families because these wrong attitudes are not being corrected in a proper way by parents.

Obedience and right attitudes are brought together in a section of scripture which emphasizes the importance God places on them. "All these curses shall come upon you and pursue you and overtake you, till you are destroyed, *because you did not obey the voice of the Lord your God, to keep his commandments and his statutes which he commanded you* [obedience]. They shall be upon you as a sign and a wonder, and upon your descendants for ever. *Because you did not serve the Lord God with joyfulness and gladness of heart* [attitude], by reason of the abundance of all things"

(Deut. 28:45-47). Obedience and right attitudes are the key issues in "training up a child in the way he should go." In this way we help our children to know the purposes of God for their lives. These purposes can be seen in the illustration below.

God's Purpose	Foolishness
1. Loving obedience—following His Son, Jesus Christ	1. Disobedience—following one's own way
2. Right attitudes—conformed to Christ's image	2. Wrong attitudes—manifestations of selfishness

EXCUSES FOR NOT DISCIPLINING*

1. "He is not old enough to understand."

If a child is old enough to know what the words "doggie" or "ice cream" or "bye-bye" mean, then he is old enough to understand the word "no." I have heard parents boast about how smart their children are: "He can wave bye-bye already," or "He can clap his hands pat-a-cake." But when it comes to disobedience and being a nuisance to other people, they say the child does not under-

*Taken from *How To Be the Parents of Happy and Obedient Children*, Published by Bible Voice, Inc., Van Nuys, CA.

stand and therefore must be tolerated. But this is merely an excuse.

2. "Oh, he is so tired today. He is always naughty when tired."

This is a commonly heard excuse for disobedience. It is remarkable that two minutes before the child disobeyed he was not tired. But after disobeying, suddenly he is "so tired." Even though the child may be tired, he can learn to control his behavior and attitude.

3. "It isn't his fault."

Johnny wants to play with a ball that sister Suzie is playing with, for example. Johnny kicks and screams, whines and fusses, crying, "I want to play with the ball."

A parent might excuse this behavior, reasoning, "If he had the ball, he wouldn't be angry. So I'll ask Suzie to give the ball to him. Then he will be happy."

Such reasoning puts the blame for Johnny's obnoxious behavior, by implication, on Suzie. If Suzie were not playing with the ball, Johnny would be good. But it is easy to see that it is Johnny's behavior which is wrong. And Johnny needs to be disciplined.

Another example would be found in the case where Johnny lies to his mother regularly. But mother blames Johnny's lying on Pete, with whom Johnny plays. Johnny learned to lie from Pete. Therefore it is not Johnny's fault.

Even though children are around others who may show poor behavior, parents still must require proper behavior from their children. The key principle here is to discipline for wrong behavior. The establishment of blame or responsibility is always difficult. It is the behavior, however, which the parent must discipline in order to control.

4. "He's this way because we are not home."

Again, this is merely an excuse for poor training at home. If you are visiting somewhere or on vacation, you must not blame the new setting for your child's disobedience and crankiness. The child must obey you wherever you are. *You* are the child's security; *your word* is to be obeyed wherever you are, whether shopping, at the zoo, or even at grandmother's house.

5. "Oh, he's just not feeling well. He's probably cutting a tooth."

Parents need to be sensitive to children's needs for proper rest and special care when they are not feeling well and of course they should not be disciplined for being sick. But disobedience cannot be excused as "not feeling well." If a child is very sick, he will be too sick to be naughty. But if the child is just down with a cold or a new tooth, the word no still must mean "no," and yes must mean "yes."

6. "Oh, he's just like his Uncle Jim. Jim has a real temper, too."

The rod of correction will deal with any hereditary trait that is not proper, even though someone in the family may not have had the rod administered. It's probably too late for Uncle Jim. But you can be sure that it's not too late for your child.

7. "He will outgrow it."

The child may outgrow the outward acts that are disobedient. But he will not outgrow the attitudes associated with that disobedience. When children start school, for example, they soon learn that if they want

to have friends they must not pinch or hit
other children. They learn to conform outwardly to certain norms of behavior. But the
attitudes which were behind the pinching
and hitting will show themselves in other
forms of aggressive behavior. And early discipline by a parent will correct these sinful
attitudes.

Key Thought

A spanking is given to correct the areas of willful disobedience and wrong attitudes.

Key Verse

"Children, obey your parents in everything, for this pleases the Lord."—Col. 3:20

Part Three

How to Give a Spanking

Parents need to understand the necessity God places on spanking and when a spanking should be given; but it is also important to know *how* to give a spanking. Some parents who say they spank their children see very little results in training them in obedience and right attitudes; the problem might be that what they mean by a spanking amounts to only one or two swats with the hand. This is not how a spanking should be given and will not produce the desired results. There are eight major areas that need to be understood in order to give an effective spanking. As Larry Christenson says in his book *The Christian Family**, "Spanking is an event," and because it is an event it needs direction and purpose.

---

*Published by Bethany Fellowship, Inc., Minneapolis, MN, 1970.

EIGHT INSTRUCTIONS FOR SPANKING

1. Use the right instrument.

"The *rod* and reproof give wisdom, but a child left to himself brings shame to his mother" (Prov. 29:15). "He who spares the *rod* hates his son, but he who loves him is diligent to discipline him" (13:24). "Folly is bound up in the heart of a child, but the *rod* of discipline drives it far from him" (22:15). "Do not withhold discipline from a child; if you beat [spank] him with a *rod*, he will not die. If you beat [spank] him with a *rod* you will save his life from Sheol" (23:13, 14).

God has instructed parents to use a stick, not the hand, when they need to lovingly correct their children with a spanking. (A rod is a *flexible* branch or twig or stick.) The hand is a part of the parent and should be used for purposes of expressing affection and loving service.

One day a father who had used his hand as an instrument for discipline reached out to his child to give him a loving embrace. Instead of responding positively to the father's gesture, the child flinched and retreated when he saw his father's arms extended toward him.

The rod is a neutral object, it has one purpose and it should have its own special identity for a child. My wife can still remember the respect she had for the "little stick" that sat on the red kitchen shelf in the Minnesota farm house where she grew up. Although she remembers having a proper fear of that stick, she did not experience fear toward her parents, only love and appreciation.

God has instructed parents to spank with a stick because in His wisdom He knows this is the most effective way of providing the loving correction children need. The reason for this is that spanking, although an outward act, ultimately deals with the heart issues within a child. A spanking is not an enjoyable experience but rather a character-changing experience. Through the pain of a spanking a child is to be brought to the place of repentance over what he or she has done wrong. A stick is the most effective instrument to spank with because its flexibility brings the greatest amount of stinging pain without the danger of physical injury. Stiff, hard objects like paddles or wooden spoons don't produce as much pain and also include the possibility of injuring a child. Belts, although flexible, are not as effective as a stick and also might cause injury.

Other forms of discipline such as putting a child in a corner, or depriving him of supper, or sending him to his room are not effective means of discipline because the issues of willful disobedience and wrong attitudes within a child's heart remain untouched. Often when children are put in corners or sent to their room, resentment and bitterness have opportunity to grow within their hearts. Harsh, unkind or belittling words such as "good-for-nothing" or "spoiled brat" are destructive to a child and must never be considered proper discipline. Even parents who would never think of spanking their children, regarding it as cruel and unjust, will speak words to them in anger, causing inner wounds that can take a lifetime to heal.

Repeatedly I hear from parents about the positive changes that have taken place in their children when they have changed to spanking them with a rod when correction was needed. For myself, it took a while to see the importance of using a rod. Now that my children are older, they have told me that they respected and feared the rod more than anything else I ever used for spanking.

It should also be noted that there may be times when spanking with a rod can leave marks on a child's bottom, especially if several spankings are needed within a brief period of time. However, these marks are temporary and should not become a source of discouragement to parents. It is better for children to carry a few temporary marks on the outside than to carry within them areas of disobedience and wrong attitudes that can leave permanent marks on their character. "Blows that wound cleanse away evil; strokes make clean the innermost parts" (Prov. 20:30).

2. Spank promptly.

A spanking should be given as soon as possible after a child has done something that needs correction. A spanking shouldn't be put off by a mother "until Daddy gets home." On the other hand, a father needs to be sure to take his responsibility in providing the correction of spanking when he is home and not leave it only to his wife. A child has the responsibility of obeying *both* parents, and both parents must see that discipline is given when needed. In God's order for the home, it is important for a husband to give his wife back-up support in order for her to effectively carry out her responsibility of discipline.

One reason why a spanking needs to be given promptly is that if delayed it would be easy for younger children to forget the reason for the discipline. If a two-year-old refuses to sit still in church and is spanked when the family gets home instead of being taken out during the service for a spanking, the purpose and meaning of that spanking is lost. A child is left very confused about what his parents really expect of him.

A spanking needs to be given promptly because of the negative issues that can develop in the heart of a child. It is easy for hardness or resentment or bitterness to grow if discipline is delayed. "Because sentence against an evil deed is not executed speedily, the heart of the sons of men is fully set to do evil" (Eccles. 8:11). "Discipline your son while there is hope; do not set your heart on his destruction" (Prov. 19:18).

A family is on their way for a day of fun at the park and a child becomes disobedient in the car; a parent should not say, "When we get home you're going to get a spanking!" This can create a weight on a child's spirit which will affect his entire day. Children need the release that a spanking brings. A spanking should never be "held over" a child's head.

3. Find a private place.

Spanking is a private issue between parent and child. Its purpose is correction, not embarrassment. Before a spanking is given a parent should take the child to a place where privacy can be insured. If a parent is away from home and a spanking is needed, time should be taken to find a private place. This may mean interrupting some activity, such as shopping; but as children come to realize that their parents consider training more important than personal activity, they will quickly learn that obedience is expected also when they are away from home.

One day my wife was at a park for a picnic with some friends and their children. During the day, one of the children became disobedient and needed a spanking. There were no private rooms at the park, so my wife's friend took her son into their van, closed the doors, and gave him the spanking he needed. It may not have been the most convenient, but it did provide seclusion. "Discipline your son, and he will give you rest; he will give delight to your heart" (Prov. 29:17).

4. Clarify the issue.

Before a spanking is given, it is important to make sure the child understands the reason for the spanking, in order to bring that child to a place of repentance for the particular issue involved. When God brings correction to His spiritual children He is always very specific about the issue. He never is vague or secretive about discipline. When King David sinned, God sent a prophet to confront David about the matter in a way David could understand. (See 2 Samuel 12.) Sin needs to be exposed and brought into the light. The natural tendency of the heart is to hide and cover up sin, but "he who confesses and forsakes them will obtain mercy" (Prov. 28:13).

Children need to understand that a spanking is not an attack against them personally but is correction for what they have done wrong. It is selfishness that hinders a child's self-esteem, not the correction of selfishness.

When explaining the reason for a spanking to a child, a parent can use simple and direct wording. The explanation should always be directed to what the child did. A parent should avoid vague comments such as, "Was that a nice thing to do?" or "How could you do that to me?" or "What would Daddy think?" These statements may appeal to a child's reason or emotions but do not appeal to the heart. It is best to quickly identify the wrong: "Mommy said 'no' and you disobeyed." "You were told to stop fussing," or, "You lied about taking a cookie." If a parent is uncertain about the facts of the incident, ask the child, "What did *you* do?" Often children, in an attempt to hide their sin, will try and shift the blame by telling a parent what someone else did. Sometimes a parent may have to wait awhile to find out what "really happened," but the truth will usually come to light eventually.

5. Get into a good position.

Often parents are unable to give an effective spanking because their children are not in the proper physical position to receive one. A child over a parent's knee may work fine when the child is young, but it is better to have older children simply bend over a chair or a bed.

A proper position also reflects an attitude of willingness to receive correction. Children who fight a spanking by kicking or twisting or blocking the spanking with their hands need to learn to submit to correction. One day when my daughter was still a preschooler she began to fight the spanking I was about to give her. I had never experienced this before and wasn't sure how I should handle it. A few days later while I was at work, my wife experienced the same struggle when she went to spank our daughter for disobedience. Several days later as I continued to search for the answer to this problem, I came across Proverbs

15:10: "There is severe discipline for him who forsakes the way; he who hates reproof will die." In this verse I saw the seriousness of rebellion against correction. I realized it needed to be dealt with as a separate issue in my daughter's life. I had a talk with her and explained that I didn't want her to fight a spanking if she needed one. If she did, I would need to spank her separately for her fighting. It took several spankings after this warning, but the result was a change in her attitude toward discipline. Instead of fighting and resisting a spanking, she took a posture that revealed an inward attitude of willingness to receive correction. This change made the entire issue of discipline so much easier on my wife and me, and on my daughter, and it was responsible for bringing a special sweetness and happiness into her entire disposition.

6. Spank the proper area.

God has given parents the perfect area on which to administer a spanking—the child's bottom. It is a safe place because it is well cushioned, yet it is a highly sensitive area. In order for a spanking to be effective,

good contact is important. If a younger child
has on several layers of diapers, or an older
child has on heavy jeans, a spanking will not
be effective. Parents, however, need to use
practical wisdom regarding how much
clothing to remove when spanking an older
child. Remember, a spanking is not intended to embarrass or humiliate.

Once my wife needed to give our young
son a spanking. She was in a hurry to go
somewhere, and didn't want the spanking to
take up a lot of time. She took him into the
bedroom, had him bend over the bed, and
quickly gave him a spanking. When she finished he turned to her and said, "Mommy,
could you spank me again? Only this time
let me pull down my jeans. It didn't hurt
enough." I was as surprised as my wife was
when I found out about the incident. But it
helped us to realize how much children need
effective discipline in order to bring them
release.

7. Wait for the proper cry.

The purpose of a spanking is to bring a
child's heart to a place of repentance. Repentance means having a change of mind

towards the wrong that was done, having genuine sorrow over that issue. This is different from remorse, which often occurs in children when they are put in a corner or denied a privilege. This type of discipline generates a feeling of being sorry for getting caught instead of being sorry for what was done.

Swats or slaps are not spankings. They only create anger or resentment in children and will not bring them to a place of repentance. A spanking needs to be hard enough and long enough to bring a repentant cry, a cry that says, "I'm sorry." A parent will be able to discern in a child's cry when he or she has broken and come to repentance over an issue. A repentant cry is different from a cry of anger or protest, which usually occurs at the beginning of a spanking. It is not a "fakey" cry which children sometimes give to get out of a thorough spanking; children will even scream when a parent starts a spanking. This is usually because they've learned that a parent will stop when they cry that way.

The Bible warns fathers not to provoke their children to anger. "Fathers, do not provoke your children to anger, but bring them up in the discipline and instruction of the Lord" (Eph. 6:4). In *The Christian Family*, Larry Christenson points out that one way a father can provoke children to wrath is by failing to bring them to repentance during a spanking. This principle can be seen in the illustration below.

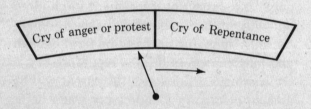

The purpose of a spanking is to move the needle up to a cry of repentance. If a spanking stops too soon, a child will remain only angered.

Exactly how long and how hard a spanking needs to be in order to bring a repentant cry is a matter for the parent to determine. It can vary, depending on the sensitivity of the child's will.

8. Have a period of reconciliation.

One time after spanking our first child, I came back to the living room to resume what I was doing. My wife looked at me and said, "You're not done yet."

"What do you mean?" I asked.

"You've left your son back in the bedroom in tears," she said. "You need to go finish the job."

I knew what she meant. I headed back to the bedroom and spent some important and needed time with him.

After correction, a parent needs to allow a child to cry for a reasonably short amount of time. Then a child should be told to stop crying and be brought under control. If parents leave the room immediately after a spanking and a child is left in tears, those tears can quickly turn into self-pity. When this happens children will usually go looking for sympathy from someone, most likely the other parent. This will not only hinder a child's repentance but create an opportunity for a child to divide the parents by working one against the other.

The period of reconciliation after a spanking provides a special time of love and intimacy to take place between a parent and a child. It gives comfort and reassurance to a child. It also helps to bring a child into self-control and freedom. The time a parent spends with a child after a spanking assures him that the issue is dealt with and over. It is in the past and is not something that will be nagged about or held against him. This can be reinforced by the parent through loving, reassuring embraces and a brief time of prayer.

Also, the time a parent spends with their children after spanking will help confirm to the parent that the child's heart has truly been brought to repentance. This can be done by instructing children to make any needed steps of restitution. If they have shown a wrong attitude to someone, they should go back and say, "I'm sorry. Will you forgive me?" If they disobeyed in some way, they need to go back and do what they were asked to do. This will bring children back into a positive direction of obedience and proper attitude. "Bear fruits that benefit repentance" (Luke 3:8).

Key Thought

A spanking must be long enough
and hard enough to bring a child
to a place of repentance.

Key Verse

"For the moment all discipline
seems painful rather than pleasant;
later it yields the peaceful fruit of
righteousness to those who have
been trained by it."—Heb. 12:11

In Conclusion...

As children learn to obey their parents they will become truly happy children. Happiness or contentment is a fruit of obedience. Through spanking, a child is trained to have not only correct outward actions but correct inward attitudes as well. A spanking is the most loving form of discipline because it truly frees a child from inward guilt. A child that does not know this freedom will easily develop a fussy or cranky disposition. Through spanking, children will come to experience a freedom from selfishness that will allow their personality, and the gifts God has given them, to *blossom*. A correctly administered spanking will break the rebellion and stubbornness in a child's will but will not break his spirit. Children who are properly disciplined by spanking know that their parents love them and will have a healthy and proper self-image. It is unkind words and actions by parents that can crush a child's spirit and self-esteem.

Spanking also develops the proper kind of fear in children—not a fear of parents, but a fear of evil. "The fear of the Lord is hatred of evil" (Prov. 8:13). Children fear parents who wrongly react to them in anger, not those who discipline them in love.

Finally, it is vital for parents to develop a *consistency* with each other in spanking. To be consistent, parents must work together and be in unity. They must agree upon what issues they will spank the children for, and each must back the other up in these decisions. Otherwise children will work one parent against the other, causing division in the home instead of unity.

Also, if parents are not consistent in the reasons *why* they spank and *when* they spank, the development of the fruits of happiness and obedience in children will be hampered. Children will become insecure and confused because they won't know where they stand on specific issues, and they won't know what's really expected of them. Someone has said, "Young children don't care which house rules parents have, but they do want to know what those rules are."

Happy children are those who know where they stand and what is expected of them. Obedient children are those who know their parents mean what they say when they say it. They know that no means "no" and yes means "yes," today as well as tomorrow. Happy and obedient children are the result of parents who do not neglect or resent the responsibilities God has given them in training up their children in the way they should go. "Even a child makes himself known by his acts, whether what he does is pure and right" (Prov. 20:11).

Key Thought

An obedient child is a happy child—a happy child is an obedient child.

Key Verse

"Children, obey your parents in the Lord, for this is right. 'Honor your father and mother' (this is the first commandment with a promise), that it may be well with you and that you may live long on the earth!"—Eph. 6:1-3

A Personal Note

If you have discovered some areas in your life that fall short of what God desires for you to be as a parent, go before Him in prayer and ask Him to make you into the parent He wants you to be. Share with your children your desire to train them up in God's ways. In areas where you have failed them as a parent, it is best to simply humble yourself before them and ask them to forgive you. Through humility God is able to bring healing. "Before destruction a man's heart is haughty, but humility goes before honor" (Prov. 18:12). Remember, it is as we become obedient spiritual sons and daughters to our heavenly Father that we will be in a position to know what kind of parents we should be to our children.

If you have never known the spiritual new birth that makes you a part of God's family, you can experience it today. Confess your sins to God and tell Him you want to turn from following your own way to following Him. Receive His forgiveness and cleansing. "If we confess our sins, he is faithful and just, and will forgive our sins and cleanse us from all unrighteousness" (1 John 1:9). By faith open up your heart and receive His Son Jesus Christ as your own personal Savior. "But to all who received him, who believed in his name, he gave power to become children of God" (John 1:12). When you receive Him, you receive spiritual life. "He who has the Son has life" (1 John 5:12). Becoming God's spiritual son or daughter through Jesus Christ is the first and most important step in being the kind of parent your children need. Look to Him daily for your every need. He can love through you, be your patience, your wisdom and your strength.

A seminar on the subject "How To Be the Parents of Happy and Obedient Children" is conducted by the author. For information write:

Roy Lessin
Bethany Fellowship, Inc.,
6820 Auto Club Road
Minneapolis, MN 55438

TEN QUESTIONS PARENTS ASK
ABOUT SPANKING

1. *How old should a child be before a spanking is given?*

Since children develop differently, it is difficult to give an exact age in numbers as to when spanking should begin. But the following guidelines will help a parent determine the approximate time in a child's life when spanking is the appropriate response to wrongdoing.

A. A child should not be spanked until a parent is sure the child has willfully rebelled, in attitude or action, against the will of the parent.

B. By the time most children reach the age of one year, they have begun to crawl or walk. Once this mobility begins, parents will need to set down specific guidelines for the child. A child who is actually moving about the house is able to understand the meaning of the words "no" or "don't touch" or other simple directives that express a parent's will. Willful disobedience at this stage will be very easy to detect. For example, a child who is told "come here" by a parent but turns instead and goes in the opposite direction or stubbornly refuses to budge is willfully disobeying. A spanking is in order.

C. Although a small child may not be able to talk, many other forms of communication are used to express resistance to a parent's will. Some express it through a cry of complaint or anger. Others will pretend to ignore a parent. Others will stiffen their bodies. Some will pout. Others will try to push their parents away with their hands. Through any or all of these actions, a child is clearly letting it be known that he wants his own way.

D. Through the wisdom of the Holy Spirit and the natural discernment God gives to parents, they should have no difficulty determining when a child is ready for the first spanking. No one knows a child better than his parents. Parents are soon able to distinguish between a cry that comes as a result of hunger, tiredness or discomfort, as compared to a cry of anger or protest. The cry that says, "I am in pain" or "I am afraid" is different from the cry that says, "I want my own way."

2. *What age should a child be when spankings are no longer given?*

Once again, it is difficult to determine the exact age. Many people have come to believe that spankings should not be given once a child reaches the age of thirteen. Ideally, a child should not have to be spanked by the time the teenage years are reached. It would be unwise, however, to make a firm rule and say a teenager should never be spanked.

If a child has been trained with the rod of correction from his early years, the need for spankings will become less and less as the child grows older. The purpose of a spanking in the early years is to help develop a child's character in righteousness. Once this character is formed, it will be normal for a child to have good behavior. This training will also bring a child into a positive and responsive relationship with his parents.

C. S. Lovett states, "When a child is properly trained, he has to go against his own spirit to do the wrong thing. That's why God commands us to train our children—God says *train*, not teach. Teaching alone won't work. Teaching imparts knowledge; training builds character. A person won't keep from doing wrong just because he knows it's wrong. It takes the rod of correction to train someone."

Proverbs 17:10 states, "A reproof entereth more into a wise man than a hundred stripes into a fool" (KJV). The normal course of training is to develop a child's character to the place where a firm word of reproof from a parent is all that is needed to see a change in behavior. This reponse will be the result of the rod of correction.

In situations where parents have older teenagers who are rebellious, it would be best not to try to deal with the rebellion through the means of spanking. By this time much of the child's character has been formed. This does not mean there is no hope and that change can't happen, but other steps will no doubt need to be taken to see that change takes place. The causes and reasons for rebellion can be numerous. The most effective steps a parent can take are ones of humility and compassion. If a child is rebellious, it does not mean a parent has failed; however, a parent should search his own heart to determine if he has been guilty of any wrong actions or attitudes that have been a cause for the rebellion. (For example, a child's rebellion may spring from an attitude within a mother that resents the authority of her husband. Or the rebellion may have its roots in the broken promises of a neglectful father.)

If a parent detects something within himself that has given cause for rebellion, that parent should go to his teenager in a spirit of brokenness and confess his sin and ask for the teenager's forgiveness. Even if a parent senses no personal sin toward the teenager, he or she should always reach out with a heart of love and acceptance, rather than being firm and rigid in "rightness." God's desire is to bring healing and restoration to a broken family relationship, and parents should seek to be His channel of healing.

If a teenager continues in rebellion, parents need to commit him to the Lord and leave him in God's hands. God will be faithful to bring the loving chastening that is needed through situations and other people in his life. God's purpose is to restore the hearts of the children to the parents.

3. *Aren't there different types of discipline a parent can use, other than spanking, that will be just as effective in training a child in right attitudes and obedience?*

It is true that there are many approaches to child discipline today. Some believe a point or merit system should be established. Some believe a child only should be reasoned with or given various options regarding obedience. Others believe in a reward system. Still others believe privileges should be taken away, while others believe children should be put in a corner or sent to their room. Some approaches seem simple to adopt; others seem very complex. Many sound good and reasonable. None of these, however, is an effective, long-range substitute for spanking.

Scripture warns us "not to lean on our own understanding." The Scriptures do not present spanking as a good, alternative form of discipline for a parent to use; it is not presented as an option. God commands parents to spank their children if the parents truly love them. Spanking may not always agree with a parent's own reasoning or emotions; nevertheless, it should be done from the heart, out of obedience to God. Parents must believe that God's wisdom is higher than their own, and that His ways will produce the fruits of happiness and obedience in their children.

4. *Shouldn't the degree of discipline vary according to the degree of disobedience?*

This question is very closely related to the previous question. Once again, the difficulty comes when a parent tries to determine what is the proper form of discipline and how it should be administered. Spanking uncomplicates the whole issue of discipline for a parent. If a child has been willfully disobedient, that child needs to be spanked. There is only one way to give an effective spanking (see section on "How to Give a Spanking"). A spanking shouldn't be administered on the basis of "two swats for whining, three swats for hitting, five swats for lying, etc." A spanking should bring a child to a place of repentance, no matter what issue of disobedience is being dealt with.

Adopting varying forms or degrees of discipline only tends to complicate the issue and bring confusion to both the parents and the child. This can also place an unnecessary burden on a parent to act as judge in trying to determine what type of disobedience should receive what type of discipline. With that approach a parent has no absolute basis to determine whether the type of discipline being administered is fair.

5. *Why is it that some parents' children are easy to train, and others' are difficult? Aren't parents with good children at an advantage?*

First of all, no child is basically good and no child is perfect. Every child chooses selfishness even before their reason is developed. The Scriptures declare the "foolishness [the attitude to want my own way] is in the heart of every child." The disposition of a child's personality should not be confused with the disposition of his heart. Not all children express their rebellion in the same way. Some children are outwardly quiet or even naturally sweet, others are more vocal or physically active. The child that "sweetly" approaches a parent in order to get his own way is just as guilty as the child that throws a temper tantrum. Parents that have "good" children have trained them to be that way. They were not born that way.

6. *Is it wrong for a parent to show emotions when a spanking is being given?*

The display of emotion is a very real and important part of spanking. Parents are not robots. Through emotion a parent is expressing the grief that is being experienced because of the child's disobedience. This will be conveyed by the tone of a parent's voice, the expression of his face, or the tears in his eyes. This genuine grief or emotion must not be confused with selfish anger. There is a big difference between spanking a child with emotion and spanking a child with anger. Genuine grief expresses the heavenly Father's righteousness and love. The

Scriptures warn us, however, that the wrath of man (selfish anger) does not work the righteousness of God.

7. Won't spanking my child create a negative barrier between us?

The purpose of a spanking is to deal with the negative attitudes and actions in a child which are the cause of strains, tensions, and barriers within a parent-child relationship. The results of biblical discipline are always "the peaceable fruits of righteousness." Loving discipline through spanking brings a parent and child closer together instead of farther apart. By properly dealing with the negative behavior in a child, a parent is removing the hindrances to a truly *enjoyable* relationship.

8. If spanking is good and right, why is there so much controversy over it, and why are so many people against it?

One reason, of course, is the wrong association between biblical spanking, which comes from a heart of parental love, and the act of child abuse, resulting from parents whose hearts are filled with anger and frustration.

A second reason is that spanking is a revelation of God's wisdom, not man's. Often men exalt their wisdom, opinions and judgments above God's. Man, through his criticism, says, "I am more loving than God. After all, if God is love, why would He ask me to do such a thing?"

A third reason is due to Satanic opposition. Spanking is a spiritual issue. The Scripture declares, "Withhold not discipline from the child. For if you strike and punish him with the (reed-like) rod, he will not die. You shall whip him with the rod [a straight, slender stick], and deliver his life from Sheol" (Prov. 23:13, 14) Amplified. Because a spanking deals with the heart of a child and establishes godly fear and wisdom within a child, it is easy to understand why Satan would oppose it.

9. Because a parent is so much bigger and stronger than a child, isn't it cruel to spank? Also, if God is a God of love, doesn't spanking give a wrong representation of His nature?

It is important to remember that spanking is not determined by a parent's size but by his position within the family. God has placed parents over children, not to be their "big pals," but to give them the love, the teaching, the example, and the discipline they need.

There is no question that God is love, but God is also holy. Because He is love, He accepts us as His children when we receive His Son, Jesus Christ, as our Savior and Lord. Because God is holy, He seeks to change us so that we will become like Him. As His children, He wants us to be a reflection of *both* His love and His righteousness. "As he is, so are we in this present world." Since God is holy love, it is perfectly consistent with His nature to both embrace us and to chasten us.

10. *How often should a parent expect to spank a child?*
There is no set pattern. Some children will need to be spanked more often than others. At times a child may need to be spanked several times in a day. Sometimes a child may even need to be spanked more than once within a brief period, for the same issue. On the other hand, a long time period can pass without the need of a spanking. The first five years, however, are when a parent can expect the need for spanking to be the greatest.

Parents may also discover after a "season" of frequent spankings, a child will go through a "quiet" period. Then, when a child reaches a new stage of development, he will retest some of the old ground to see if things have changed in Mom or Dad's thinking. These "retesting" periods can cause a parent to become discouraged and feel like their training is not paying off. However, this disposition within a child will quickly pass if a parent remains faithful and consistent. "And let us not be weary in well doing: for in due season we shall reap, if we faint not" (Gal 6:9) KJV.

In closing, let me restate the need for keeping spanking in its proper place in the total picture of child training. Spanking is only one aspect of their training. For a parent's training to be totally effective, he needs to maintain a proper Christlike example, walk before his children in humility and love, and instruct his children in God's ways. All this can be accomplished as a parent leans his entire dependence upon the power of the Holy Spirit and, through the Spirit, draws upon the Lord's complete sufficiency.

Remember, God has not called children to be perfect, but obedient. A parent should not expect perfection from his children but, rather, obedience with a right attitude. And remember, also, that the goal and purpose of all training is to direct a child's heart and life toward Jesus Christ.

TWENTY ISSUES OF CHILD TRAINING—
FROM GOD'S VIEWPOINT AND
FROM MAN'S VIEWPOINT

"The fear of the Lord is the beginning of wisdom."

Man Says:

God Says:

1. Children should have a mind of their own and should make their own decisions regarding church and religion.

1. "My son, hear the instruction of thy father, and forsake not the law of thy mother" (Prov. 1:8) KJV.

2. Children need to be taught to be open and broadminded. There are many people that have points of view worth listening to. No one source can supply a person with what he needs. To do so would be narrow-mindedness.

2. "For that they hated knowledge, and did not choose the fear of the Lord: They would none of my counsel: they despised all my reproof. Therefore shall they eat of the fruit of their own devices" (Prov. 1:29-31) KJV.

3. Children are not affected by the TV shows, cartoons and books that they read.

3. "Keep thy heart with all diligence, for out of it are the issues of life" (Prov. 4:23) KJV.

4. It is wrong for a child to grow up with any type of fear.

4. "The fear of the Lord is to hate evil" (Prov. 8:13a) KJV.

5. If my child is able to do what he wants to do when he grows up, and is able to have financial security, he will make me happy.

5. "A wise son maketh a glad father; but a foolish son is the heaviness of his mother" (Prov. 10:1) KJV.

6. No one is going to tell me how to raise my kids.

6. "Whoever loves discipline loves knowledge, but he who hates reproof is stupid" (Prov. 12:1) RSV.

7. It doesn't really matter who my child's playmates are. They should learn to be friends with everyone.

7. "He that walketh with wise men shall be wise: but a companion of fools shall be destroyed" (Prov. 13:20) KJV.

8. I wouldn't spank my child because I love him too much. Besides, that would be cruel.

8. "He who spares his rod hates his son, but he who loves him diligently disciplines and punishes him early" (Prov. 13:24) Amplified.

9. I want my children to have what I didn't have as a child. My first priority is my family's financial security.

9. "He that is greedy of gain troubleth his own house" (Prov. 15:27a) KJV.

10. I need to act "tough" around my kids to gain their respect.

10. "Before honour is humility" (Prov. 15:33b) KJV.

11. I know my child is having some problems, but he'll outgrow them.

11. "Chasten thy son while there is hope" (Prov. 19:18a) KJV.

12. I would never spank my child because it may hurt him.

12. "The blueness of a wound cleanseth away evil: so do stripes the inward parts of the belly" (Prov. 20:30) KJV.

13. I resent having to correct my child.

13. "It is joy to the just to do judgment" (Prov. 21:15a) KJV.

14. It's not that important if I'm home with my children. A baby-sitter can take care of any problems.

14. "Train up a child in the way he should go: and when he is old, he will not depart from it" (Prov. 22:6) KJV.

15. Children are basically good: it is society and adult taboos that give them hangups.

15. "Foolishness is bound in the heart of a child; but the rod of correction shall drive it far from him" (Prov. 22:15) KJV.

16. Spanking a child is not that important. There are many more effective and kinder ways to discipline a child.

16. "Withhold not discipline from the child, for if you strike and punish him with the (reed-like) rod, he will not die. You shall whip him with rod, and deliver his life from Sheol" (Prov. 23:13, 14) Amplified.

17. I love my wife and kids. That's all that counts.

17. "Through wisdom is an house builded; and by understanding it is established" (Prov. 24:3) KJV.

18. It's important that a child learns to do his own thing. Restraints can discourage him.

18. "The rod and reproof give wisdom: but a child left to himself bringeth his mother shame" (Prov. 29:15) KJV.

19. It is good for a child to express himself when he is mad or angry.

19. "He that hath no rule over his own spirit is like a city that is broken down" (Prov. 25:28) KJV.
"An angry man stirreth up strife, and a furious man aboundeth in transgression" (Prov. 29:22) KJV.
"A fool uttereth all his mind: but a wise man keepeth it in till afterwards" (Prov. 29:11) KJV.

20. I'm afraid if I spank my child he will not like me.

20. "Discipline your son, and he will give you peace; he will bring delight to your soul" (Prov. 29:17) NIV.